THE Twisted TALE OF ADAM & EVE

BY: DR. DAN

An Inflatable Stories Publication
Thomasville, GA

InflatableStories.com

ISBN 978-0-9979039-3-5

When *The Inflated Story of Noah* released in 2016, I could not imagine the twist my life was about to take. In 2017, my long-time hobby became a full-time calling as Inflatable Stories began to blow up. Reach Your City popped into my life to help me get started, and churches and fellow believers began to reach out to me to share. These blessings allowed me to take my work to a new level.

The dream for *The Twisted Tale of Adam and Eve* began as I was finishing the Noah book, but no great project takes on air without help. My parents have been incredibly supportive over the years, particularly as Inflatable Stories took float. Many friends have helped me take balloon photos, and I am especially thankful to my friend Jonathan Miles who took part of his summer teaching break to travel with me to Europe. I will always be grateful he saw my constant detours to photograph balloons as adventures rather than annoyances.

I also want to thank *you* for reading. What began with a dream for a single book has blossomed into a vision for a series of biblically based balloon books, and perhaps even an entire bubble Bible. Readers like you are helping sculpt this dream into a reality.

In the beginning, God created the heavens and the earth....

The Universe

Cliffs of Moher, Ireland

Over seven days, God made the birds of the air, and the fish of the sea, and the animals on land.

After creating it all, God saw that it was very good, and took a day for rest.

Cliffs of Moher, Ireland

The first person God created was Adam, but God saw it was not good for one person to be alone.

God created all kinds of animals to keep Adam company and brought each of them to him to name.

Multnomah Falls, Portland, OR

The Zebra was fast and earned its stripes, bu Adam was not looking fo the best runner.

Menomonie, WI

The Lion was strong with a powerful roar, but the lion was not the helper Adam needed.

Oslo, Norway

Smoky Mountain National Park, TN

The **BEAR** could stand tall and climb really well.

But it slept too much and was not very good company.

Smoky Mountain National Park, TN

The Giraffe
was unique with a
neck that could reach
high into the trees.

But it still was not the
one Adam needed.

Saxeten, Switzerland

None of the animals would do, so God put Adam to sleep and set to work. God removed a rib from Adam and used it to form Eve.

They were so perfect for each other that they were like one person!

Nye Beach, Newport, OR

Nye Beach, Newport, OR

Thomasville, GA

Adam and Eve lived in paradise, and there was no sin in the world.

They were only given one rule: Don't eat from the tree of the knowledge of good and evil.

Mobile, AL

For a little while everything was perfect, but there was a snake in the garden who tempted Eve.

It told her she could be like God if she ate some of the forbidden fruit.

When we miss the mark in the way we love God, that is a sin. If Eve ate the fruit she would be sinning, but she could not resist.

Mobile, AL

After Eve ate the fruit, she offered some to Adam, and he made the same bad decision.

When God looked for them in the garden, they hid and made clothes for themselves. For the first time, they knew they were naked.

Sin had entered the world, and Adam and Eve had to leave the perfect garden.

Mobile, AL

Sin would get even worse.

Adam and Eve had two sons named Cain and Abel.

Cain was the oldest. He was a farmer, but Abel kept animals. One time, they each brought a gift to God from their hard work.

Cain brought something from his field and Abel brought something from his flock.

Bad Schwalbach, Germany

Bad Schwalbach, Germany

God did not like Cain's gift, but God did like what Abel offered him.

This made Cain very angry at his brother!

When we miss the mark in the way we love others, that is another kind of sin.

Bad Schwalbach, Germany

While he was angry, Cain sinned.

He tricked Abel into coming out to a field, where he thought no one could see them.

Then he killed Abel, his own brother!

Cain tried to hide what he had done so he would not get in trouble, but God knows all the good and bad things we do.

Bad Schwalbach, Germany

Bad Schwalbach, Germany

Cain did not want to face what he had done, but it was too late.

God still loved him, but the results of his sin changed his life.

Cain could not farm anymore, and he had to move away from his home. He became a wanderer.

Sin was growing in the world, but God had a plan to save us.

The plan would take time, sacrifice, and the greatest love the world has ever known. The plan was Jesus.

Bad Schwalbach, Germany

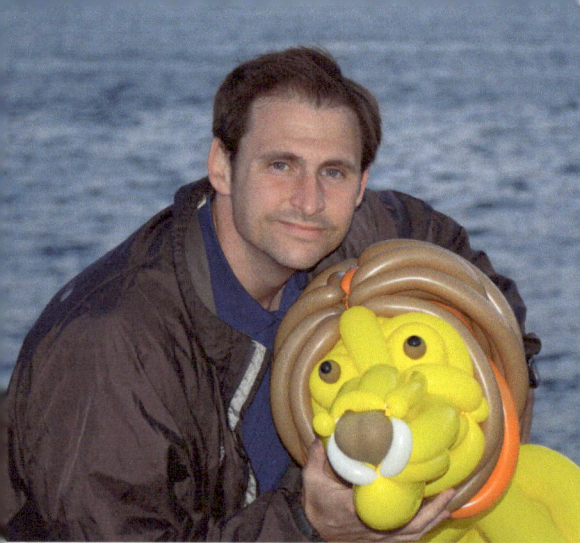

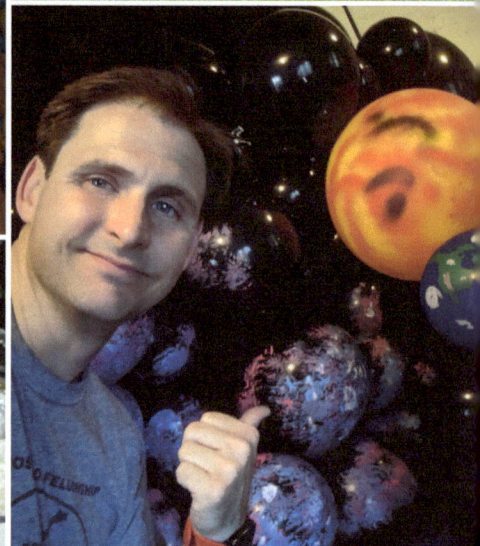

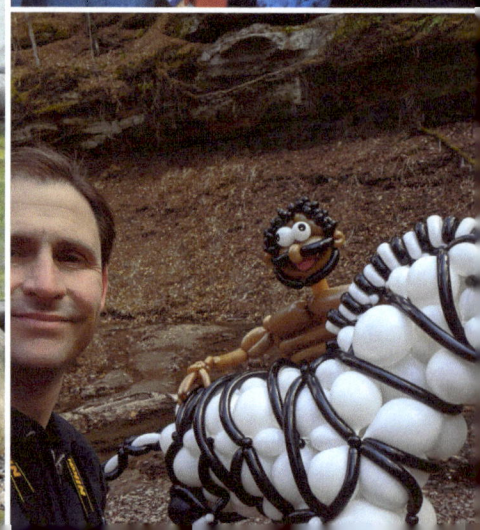

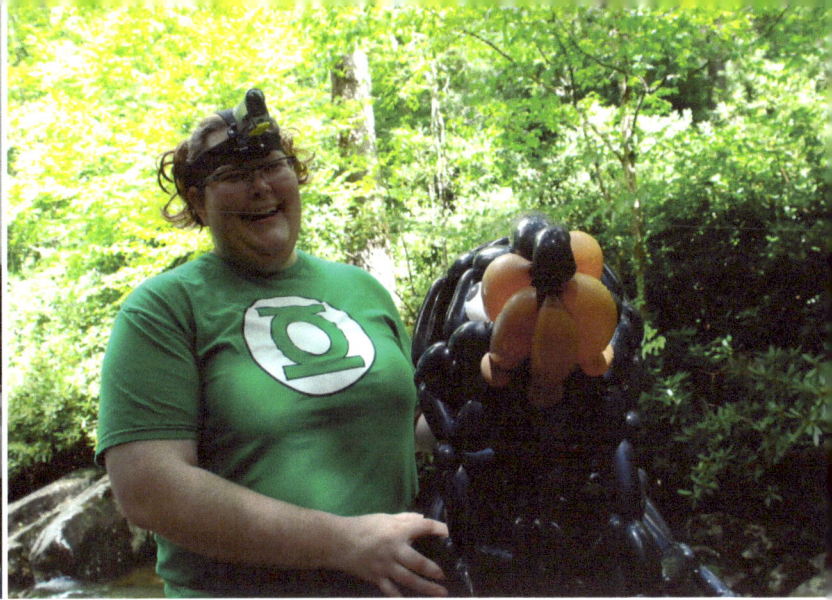

Learn more about these books,
and how you can have Inflatable Stories
at your church, by visiting
InflatableStories.com

www.ingramcontent.com/pod-product-compliance
Lightning Source LLC
Chambersburg PA
CBHW041959100426
42813CB00019B/2928